Hettie Adams & Hermione Suttner

WILLIAM STREET
DISTRICT SIX

CHAMELEON
PRESS

Text © Hettie Adams & Hermione Suttner 1988
Published by Chameleon Press
19 Estmil Road, Diep River 7800
(Postal address: PO Box 117, Plumstead 7800)
Designed by Linda Vicquery
Setting & reproduction by ProSet-Flexoplate
Printed & bound by CTP Book Printers, Parow

First edition 1988
Second impression 1989

ISBN 0 620 12476 8

BD9749

Contents

Introduction

"Things happened in William Street and I tell you it happened nowhere else."

This is the distinctive voice of Hettie Adams, who grew up in District Six, Cape Town. Today she lives in one of the city's outlying suburbs to which her people have been banished. The biblical turn of phrase is not out of place, because District Six has in this exile become Jerusalem, the lost paradise, the one they hope they will somehow regain. District Six has assumed a power which no amount of rebuilding or replanning will obscure: here is a place, once real, which has been transformed by its people's memories into myth.

But it is not an ethereal dream. District Six was an old, run down area, largely owned by absentee landlords. To the official eye it was a slum. Yet it is in the nature of such places to teem with life, providing the observer with images of variety and colour, and the inmates with sensations of human warmth and community that are emphasised by the very closeness of their neighbours. Since these neighbours are mostly in the same boat, materially speaking, the place is a great and comforting leveller. Pretensions are scorned with a healthy awareness of what is genuine: family ties, friendship, the sharing of food and comfort in bad times, and an ability to enjoy carnival times without inhibition.

This is the way Hettie Adams begins her story: with the sound of the 'goema' (pronounced 'gooma' as spelled in the text) and all the exuberance of holidays in William Street. Gadidja and her drum, the coons and their 'klopse' bands, dominate the scene with insistent sound and the vibrancy of their bright satin clothes. It is a world where the 'moffie' Rachmat (here the word denotes not so much a homosexual as an effeminate man, or a transvestite) is mocked but not excluded; he is an insider, one of the crowd. In District Six no one – neither the moffie nor the gangster – is seen as the outsider. District Six is a microcosm of the ideal world, a richly human place where everyone is welcome if he or she will only share – music, joy, outrageous clothes, or fish, bright Malay cookies, the bread and polony of an old, poor spinster, Dadda's ceremonial watermelon served on a big brass tray.

Dadda himself is a central figure in Hettie's story. Of all her family he most clearly stands for the blend of love and authority that are indivisible. Hettie's father shouts and beats his children, but they know he is merely doing his best to keep the family together after their mother's death. To Dadda there is a constant threat in the very life of District Six, where neighbours are not all poor and 'decent' – many are 'dronkies' (alcoholics) and 'skollies' (hoodlums, gangsters).

But Dadda's children, as Hettie testifies, are in fact already excellent judges of what is important in life: Hettie will play happily on the sly with the children of dronkies; she will talk to the gangsters, whose youthful insecurity she instinctively understands. But she will mock the Society Ones for their delusions of grandeur – the smart clothes that mean their children cannot play with others in the street, the stiff patent leather shoes where others go barefoot or shod in their 'takkies' (canvas shoes) or 'sloffies' (slippers). And she will bitterly condemn the Sly One for hypocrisy, for her failure to share her home and her husband's funeral (a great communal occasion in District Six).

Dadda is also blind to even more important issues. Unlike Hettie, he never recognises the goodness of Ruby, the daughter in law who comes to live in a 'hokkie' – a shed – in the family's back yard. In a country where colour is counted as an index of worth, Ruby's blackness obscures what a child can see clearly. And it is Dadda's sons who must warn him of the approaching cruelty of apartheid – segregation endorsed by law. Fortunately (so Hettie feels) Dadda dies without being forced to witness the demolition of District Six.

The forced removal of a whole community is a traumatic event. District Six – a mixed area where many different groups lived together – was officially proclaimed a white 'Group Area' in 1966. Demolition began in 1968. By the early 80s the buildings – houses, cinemas, shops, legendary trysting places like the Seven Steps of Hanover Street, everything except a few stubbornly surviving churches and mosques – were gone. The land lay empty, levelled, divested of its street signs – William Street had vanished without trace. People returning, as if to worry an old scar, were lucky if they found a lamp post or a paving stone to identify their past lives.

Hettie tells the story of the diaspora as she saw it: in fragments, as the breaking up of families, the separation of friends, as loss of contact and of continuity, the loss of places of worship, and of happily remembered entertainment – the rowdy bioscopes (cinemas), the communal picnics by the sea. The action of the bulldozers as they came to level the sites of demolition merely set a final nightmarish seal, because it was so visible, on what was already painfully clear: the basic powerlessnes of the community.

Now, split, scattered, impoverished (in that most important of ways, spiritually), the long gone community occasionally regathers at a funeral, or a musical that portrays the good old days. Many of them have experienced an alienation and a disorientation, in their new impersonal homes, which has robbed them of the belief that life is meaningful.

Hettie's story is only one of many, but it seems especially moving, funny and sad by swift turns. In a fruitful collaboration, Hermione Suttner has caught Hettie's words with a particularly faithful ear, preserving the unique flavour of the Cape dialect with its unfussy blend of Afrikaans and English, its disdain for the 'correct' forms of verbs, and its own ripe slang. Unobtrusively shaping the story into chapters, she has let Hettie's vibrant portrait of District Six speak for itself, as it so memorably does. Then – at first muffled, later more insistently, like the recurring beat of Gadidja's drum – the warning notes begin to intrude which signal the end of Hettie's world. The restraint of both women in their telling of the story is one of the most moving features of the book.

Names and even characters have been changed, without however altering the atmosphere or dimming the essential truth of the place that was William Street, District Six.

Lynne Bryer
Cape Town 1988

List of illustrations

The photographs in this book have been used with the kind permission of the people and institutions indicated. The help and enthusiasm of Dr K Schoeman and Arlene Fanarof of the South African Library, and of photographer Willie de Klerk, is in particular gratefully acknowledged.

1 Gadidja

Gooma, gooma, the gooma is going. Gadidja is beating the gooma.

It is the first day of New Year, and if we in William Street did not have the gooma, it wouldn't be New Year.

Gadidja sits astride her big drum, her family come outside to their stoep which is on the pavement, they gather around her. When Gadidja gets tired one of her daughters takes over. Gadidja smiles and her big teeth are flashing. More and more people are gathering around and Gadidja is inspired.

'Die gooma speel,' I shout to my brother Okkie and in a minute we are sitting next door at the Malays. 'Look people from all the streets are coming and calling others to join, they come dancing towards Gadidja, hey, Okkie, here come the dronkies and the skollies.'

Gadidja was so popular and you could hear her from where you lived in District Six.

People would get off the ships and somehow the word would get around Gadidja was playing, and that was one thing tourists would come and see and hear.

They spoke about her in England:

'Like our Cockneys, so lively, such repartee.'

'Better than the Rio carnival.'

And the people were shouting: 'Haai, gooi daardie number, gooi, gooi.'

I have new takkies on, painted ones, and I'm swinging my legs and I'm clapping my hands to the gooma.

There comes the tall moffie Rachmat, he's got a girl's name, so tall and skinny like a stick. Rachmat stays near us, he is always there as soon as he hears the gooma and comes dancing up with his turban, shorts, earrings, sloffies and bangles. 'F___ you skollies,' he shouts as we touch him.

'Gooi maar, booi maar, dancing legs going like sticks, dance faster,' they egg Rachmat on, and on and on he goes till five in the morning.

'Haai, moenie jou onbeskof hou nie,' he shouts at us as we want to dance with him.

'Ma, play "Daar kom die Alabama",' Rachmat shouts to Gadidja.

The knot of his turban hanging down the side of the neck flies in the air as he dances.

Rachmat was a very shy person, but he knows the skollies well and goes to their houses. It was strange how he met his death later. A bus went over him. How that bus never missed him I don't know, he was so tall.

My mother always used to help sew the coon costumes at Gadidja's house, and their sons were in the Malay choir. They were one big, busy, happy family, and there was always something going on. A wedding or engagement, or a birth, besides all the Malay holidays and festivals. I loved them and at their holidays like Labarang I too would get special treats. They would come into the streets and dish out sandwiches or cookies or koeksusters, and even if there was a funeral or a wedding I would get a barkat – a little brown packet with brightly iced cookies or coconut sweets, or spiced biscuits, or jam tarts. Often after a funeral they would have a 'food night', then I would eat curry meat with dishes of carrots and peas and rice.

'Salaam Alaikom' (Peace be with you) they always said, and we all said back, 'W'alaikom Salaam' (and with you be peace also).

It was like our house. Something was always going on in our house, and there was always something happening in William Street.

The Malay choirs walked around from house to house where they would get tea and cake. They would start on New Year's Eve, then the next day they march along the streets, blowing their saxophones and strumming their banjos, and then they stop and sing. They walk and sing again, and on the second New Year's day, getting no sleep, then every Saturday again for the whole month of January, in the afternoons, they go out marching in their costumes, singing with us children following them.

From Gadidja's house came her daughter Miriam's two sons, and from our house my brothers Magpie (Stan) and Leonard (Lenny) who were in the 'Bits and Pieces'.

This band was like individuals, one klopse would wear a sailor suit, one would have a dress on, each can bring their own clothes. One had a wedding dress on, they wore wigs and little hats on their heads with flowers in it and make-up to make the people laugh , like moffies.

To me, lying in bed at night, hearing those choirs, and finally falling asleep to those sounds, that was William Street.

New Year us girls have new dresses on and we take benches and

13

chairs to Caledon Street and sit there and wait for the coons to come home down Hanover Street, and we stay there till nine at night, and then it's finished.

The big celebration for us is the coon carnival. Gadidja's family, as all the Malay families, started to bake before, busy with curries, briyani, tomato bredies, snoek koppe – the whole street is busy buying up snoek, cook the heads with onions and chillies or smoored with cabbage! That is how Ruby makes it and what I like best.

Ruby is my sister-in-law and the person I love the best in the world. She is a wonderful woman.

Things happened in William Street and I tell you it happened nowhere else.

2 Our family

I was born in William Street. Actually our house was in a lane just off William Street, and if I looked out from our house I could see the bioscope opposite, the National.

Our house belonged to whites, Jews; there was a lot of Jews, and when I was older I used to go and pay the rent once a month for my Dadda. I had to walk to Castle Bridge and just where it turns off, that was where there was an office and that was where I paid.

There were twelve of us in our house in William Street.

We had a double storied house, and downstairs the first room off the passage was for us girls. I have two sisters older than me, the eldest, Cilla, the one who only liked to go out, she likes bioscope, parties, boxing, and she should have been like a mother, but Rosie, the second eldest sister, she was like my mother. She didn't go out to work, she must keep house, but that was later. Rosie did the cooking and everything, and stayed home.

Sammy was the eldest of us all, and my mother's favourite. My father had no specials.

My sisters and I slept in one big double bed in the front room, it was a big brass bed with knobs on it. Dadda used to polish it every Saturday.

My sisters slept at the top and I slept with my head at the bottom and I crawled in between them, my feet were always nice and warm between them.

I had lots of brothers, but Sammy was my favourite and the nicest. There was:
Sammy
Cilla
Leonard
Rosie
Albert
Stan
Kevin
Okkie
Anne Hathaway – that's me, Hettie
Tommy

I must explain about my name.

My mother was Eleanor Cloete from Namaqualand. She was my father's second wife. He had no children with his first wife – he divorced that wife when he came out of the army, she was jolling around while he was away.

My mother was white, so white, and all her family was white. Maybe she had a coloured father, I don't know, perhaps a Baster, because they were half-white. My mother's cousins are mainly married to whites, one cousin married a high-up man in China or Japan, her picture was in the paper, she is beautiful. The other sister started jolling with the manager of the bioscope and they ran away together, they went to England. Her photo used to hang in our passage until the day we left William Street.

One day when my mother was pregnant she got a postcard from England. It read: 'Everything is all right. Love Linda.'

After all those years, my mother was so excited. But there was no address, just the English stamp. And the picture was pretty, a cottage with a garden: Anne Hathaway's cottage.

'A real English name,' said Dadda. He was so impressed he took the postcard down to the office when he went to register the baby's birth.

That baby was me. I was called Anne Hathaway Adams. Those people who fill in forms are so ignorant it's a wonder they didn't fill in the 'cottage' too.

But the name was too smart to last. Everyone called me Hettie.

My mother was a tall woman and she walked up straight. My father was also tall, and he walked up straight too. That must have been because of all the days in the army. He was decorated for bravery, I think he fought on horseback, charging with swords somewhere in France. He had lots of medals, and it's a pity that Okkie and I gave his medals to Jacob, our neighbour, for his horse Prins, that was after Okkie got tired of wearing them.

My mother worked at the docks with my father at the cold storage, they were foremen at the fruit packing. Often they had to work at night and I would be in bed and hear a lorry stop and drop them off at home. They would jump down and then a bag of oranges or apples would be handed to them for us.

At the back of our house we had a long table under a big fig tree and in summer sometimes we'd all eat there, even our boarders. We had boarders downstairs in one room off the kitchen where a Malay family lived, a husband and wife and their son and daughter. They rented the room and cooked their own food there. They were dronkies but they knew their limit, they knew how far they could go with my father. On Friday nights they played their guitar, sometimes the husband, sometimes the wife, and they'd sing. Rosie also used to go into their room on Friday nights and sing with them. Their children were my age.

When we ate outside then Rosie would help my mother in those days and bring out the food on trays, we'd be a lot of people, and then I don't feel like going out in the street and running around. I stay there and have tea out of nice cups and saucers and little teaspoons.

All the boys slept in one room at the end of the passage.

Sometimes my brothers would start practising a month before New Year and I would lie in bed at night and hear them singing. Nine or ten of the boys – my brothers and friends – they would get together and sing twice a week. I went to sleep with just singing voices.

My mother used to visit often at Gadidja's. At first I was shy to visit with her because there were always so many people there and new ones coming as more sisters married and more babies came, and they are all growing and growing. They were a happy family – Gawa, Eisa, Lena, Miriam, Salie, Abrahim and Farouk. All the sisters' husbands came to live there.

My mother used to help Gadidja make the clothes before the carnival, I used to look inside and see them hanging up, all the lovely colours in satins and silks.

If I said that I was shy at Gadidja's house, I must tell you that as I grew older I lost that shyness, everyone made you part of the family, and I could just take one of those bright pink or yellow or mauve cookies on the kitchen table if I wanted one, and simply sit down and eat a meal with the family if I felt like it.

My sister Cilla worked at Back's clothing factory and then at Rex Trueform, so Rosie was at home that day I came from school, she told me my mother had gone to hospital because she had a leaking heart.

It was the three weeks school holidays, about one month later, that Sammy came home from work while us youngest ones were playing about and he told us they sent a message to him – he was a cleaner at the supreme court – that our mother wanted to see us. So Sammy washed us, dressed us nicely and took us, that is, Tommy, me and Okkie, by bus to Groote Schuur hospital to see her. There was a screen around my mother and tubes everywhere into her, but my mother was still smiling at us through all those tubes.

18

My mother died and we had the funeral. Two family cars took us children, but the men and women walked behind the coffin to the station; they walked from District Six to Cape Town station.

My mother died at Groote Schuur, but they brought the corpse in the coffin to our house the day before the funeral. First it was put in our room in the front and us girls moved to the back room with the boys, the boys had to sleep on the floor.

The next night when we went back to our room we were frightened because the coffin had been there.

In the boys' room first me and Cilla slept on the floor on a mattress and then Rosie joined us. I was so scared I cried: 'Ek is die kleinste, I'm the baby, I must be in the middle,' and I went on like that till late at night, till the brothers moved to the floor and us girls went on the beds, then I wanted to be in the corner and Rosie had to sleep with me. It was so strange that night having our mother at home, but she was dead.

At Cape Town station the coffin was put on to the train and on to Maitland. The men carried the coffin from there to the cemetery. We all wore black bands around our arms.

I can remember my father standing so upright there at the graveside. He never cried. He was like a real soldier.

And from then on my father became like a mother. He did all the things a mother should do, like wash us at night, brush my hair, make sure we have sandwhiches for school, so we never missed my mother even though I was six years old.

My father never liked being away from the house except when he went to work, and even lunch times he tried to get to the house to check up on what was going on. He was strict, and that was right, very strict, he could hit us hard, and my brothers even though they were big, had to be in early and be respectful. I loved my father.

But it was funny. The man who boarded with us upstairs, Issy Karstens, he died not long after my mother died.

He had water, and was all swollen up, and when he died the coffin could not be taken up those narrow stairs, so they brought him down on a stretcher. And we were all standing downstairs in the passage watching when they came down, and halfway down they let him drop. We all jumped and screamed as he went falling off, sliding, and bang went his head.

That day we all ran from the house into the street.

There was always something happening at our house.

3 Dadda

I think Dadda got shell shock, and sometimes when he was in a good mood like on Fridays or Saturdays, he stayed at home and used to sing the army songs.

I don't understand that my father never got a pension, he had that steel box full of medals, lots of them with coloured ribbons. He even saw the woman who turned to salt, from Sodom and Gomorrah, maybe it was in Egypt.

He used to put me on his knees sometimes and tell us army stories, but not often. He thought he was still in the army the way he brought us up. There was a big photo of him in uniform with his medals on; he was a good father, he ran the whole house.

I don't know what happened to that big photo nor to his medals after Prins wore them.

When we moved out of William Street, and the Group Areas people came, and the council inspectors just came and went, they didn't say anything, just took photos and were writing, witnessing that we were going to go, somehow in that confusion the medals went, and the photo too, and the brass bed, and the lovely old enamel basin and jug, and our old-time dressing table with all the little mirrors, and lots more things.

I dream about the brass bed and the old dressing table . . .

With my father's army training he had to be obeyed. When he was in the kitchen us children in the other rooms would say: 'Die ou is daar binne, talk softly, don't say rude words,' in that way we were scared of him.

And none of my brothers ever brought girls to the house, except Sammy, when he brought Ruby home, as his wife.

All the people respected my father, when he walked up the road everyone would greet him and he would just nod his head, he always wore a hat. 'Good evening Mr Adams,' and he would touch his hat, and give a crooked smile, and go to work.

In our house, it was Leonard, the third eldest, it was his job to clean the big coal stove and he must light it. He must keep the toilet in the yard clean and sweep every day.

'Jy maak daardie stove skoon, sien dat die yard skoon is,' Dadda

was talking to Lenny. Lenny just nods his head and looks mocking.

Stan and Okkie washed up at night.

Dadda did everything else for us, got hot water to wash us, and in the morning he would get up at four and go to the big coal stove with the big chimney and put on water and make a big pot of moer coffee. And then he gives my sister Cilla coffee first for she leaves early. Then I hear him sweep the lane – it's a big house – I hear the broom going.

That big cast-iron black pot was always standing on the stove with boiling water in it, the coal stove was always burning.

Dadda cleans the mirrors, the brass lamps, the brass bed with the knobs on it every Saturday morning.

Dadda would come in at midnight and check up on each child in bed; taking his oil lamp just like Florence Nightingale, he would come to each bed and then after that he would lock the front door and no one was allowed into the house after that. No one was allowed to sleep out, not even the big ones. No matter what night of the week, all of us had to be home before twelve.

Dadda didn't have friends at the house. Sundays he loved. He would sit at that window and look at us while we played. Other children mustn't fight with us. We used to play in the yard, mommy and daddy, or shop shop, but we must not complain that children hit us because then he comes and hits us. He doesn't want to know. 'Jy skreeu met jou bek soos 'n straat meid,' he'd say to me, but he liked to watch us play.

Sundays, summer Sundays, he buys us the biggest watermelon. We stand outside and eat it because he doesn't want all the pips in the kitchen. We had a big kitchen table and there on a big brass tray Dadda cut up the watermelon beautifully, everyone gets his share of the crown and a piece besides that.

Christmas time Dadda has puddings made and he lets my sister Rosie bake special cakes and he buys us girls just one little dress. But the house next to us in the yard, the Society Ones, the Simonses – there were three girls and a boy, Joan, Noreen, Gloria and Peter – they were dressed beautifully, with golden ribbons. We never got jealous, in any case, they were so boring, always with socks and shoes and every time a clean dress, they never got dirty, and they weren't like the other English speakers, they didn't even have a wireless, and they had to be in at six o'clock in the evening.

At Christmas time we got our dress and shoes. And the Society Ones didn't know how to enjoy themselves. Even if they had frills and curls and gloves and bags, their mother Amina made their dresses. Dadda bought ours. Even if we only got one dress a year we were so proud that we put it on straight away and went and sat outside.

But that was one thing we all liked to do in District Six, to sit and see what others wore – and we all liked to admire everyone else. 'Dis a mooi sari,' or 'Kyk daardie patent skoene.'

The Simon's children always wore shoes. I used to wear little plaits with ribbons and go barefoot. The first half of school I always wore shoes because I still had my shoes from Christmas, but if my shoes broke in the middle of the year you went without until Christmas time again. Then once again I'd get a new dress and new shoes, and once again we were so excited for this little dress, it was like gold.

When Ruby started charring in Sea Point she bought me a blouse and shorts and rings, and there I sat outside, barefoot. But then I loved to go and sit with the Society Ones, just to show them, unless I'm busy playing in the street, and of course I won't play in the street in my bought clothes.

Usually I was playing either hopscotch or cricket, or just running wild in the street.

All the children used to come and play in the dining room, but we move out before five when Dadda is coming home, we are all scared of him; if we made a big mess there he'd hit us and we run like the devil.

When me and my two brothers fight, Dadda comes with a sjambok: 'Waar is die sjambok, julle baklei!' Into the lane we'd all run, then into the street.

Every morning Dadda filled the jug which stood in our bedroom with hot water and poured it in the enamel basin and washed my face and hands with a flannel wash cloth and brought me some coffee.

The diningroom had a flat roof and a stained glass section in it. We loved to climb up on that roof and lie on our stomachs and look through there down into the diningroom, there was always someone in the room and we just liked to look. It was Okkie and me that used to lie there, quiet, just looking.

Dadda moved with the boys to the back room when my mother died.

I am always fighting, so Dadda always wants to hit me. Once I threw my coffee and I ran in the street. It's nine o'clock that night and my sister Rosie comes to look for me: 'Dadda is sleeping, come home.'

I was in bed: 'Oh God, here comes Dadda!' I moved right to the bottom of the bed, but he just hit and he got me on my head. I thought: 'That's my hiding for the day.' I crept to my sister's feet, wriggled myself down the bed, comforting myself by feeling her body against mine, I am so frightened.

Dadda hit me other times too. He came to look at midnight at our bed and did not see me. In the morning he just started hitting me, saying I spent the night out. Then Rosie said: 'Dadda, sy was in die bed,' and she made Dadda come and look. I had rolled myself in the feather eiderdown and he didn't see me, but if he felt he was wrong he didn't say so, for there I was all the time; but that Saturday he gave me money for bioscope before I cut his toe nails.

Dadda drinks his coffee early in the morning in a big mug, then he goes to buy bread. That Indian shop knows the people have to go to work early so they are open very early. Dadda comes back with three big loaves, butter, cheese, and puts it down and makes sandwiches. Then he wakes us all up: 'Opstaan, six o'clock!' Then he starts getting us three young ones ready, washed and dressed.

There were no fridges in the house so we bought our food fresh every day.

Somehow they say I always made trouble. If my brothers just say 'boo' to me I say: 'Ek sal vir Dada sê,' then he shouts at them. I could not stand them teasing me.

Every Friday Dadda buys us packets full of peanuts, and in his pockets were sweets. We would stand around him and wait for our goodies. Then he would go out just for one hour to a friend in Caledon Street who has a shop and come back with lots of fruit.

And on Saturdays Dadda goes to the bar just for one tot, then he comes home like an old woman who likes to be home.

I had to cut Dadda's toe nails and then he promises to give me the money for bioscope, but he falls asleep and I start crying, I can hear the bioscope starting: 'It's starting,' I try to wake him up, but he doesn't want to wake and give me money.

So I run to the old spinster I shop for and cry, and she gives me five pennies to go to bioscope.

4 Bioscope

We make such a noise in bioscope, even when the film is showing, we were so noisy and talking so loud. All the dronkies' children and the whole gang of us went together.

There were two bioscopes: I liked the National bioscope better than the one Mrs Kaplan had. Hers was only a twopenny bioscope, but we sat on long benches and she pushed us up with a long stick, prodding us closer and closer together, we were so squashed, but we shouted and screamed there too.

My brother Okkie used to sell icecream with chocolate at the National, and we had false money, I think it was money from the war from other countries, and we would wait for the lights to go off and then buy from Okkie. Okkie used to get tips from some people but he was always short, it was the stuff we gave him, he always had to pay in.

And we shouted as we saw different people come in: 'There goes the baker's son,' and 'There goes the chicken woman's daughter,' they were Jews.

The Gordins had the Golden Bakery. It was so called because old man Gordin who was from Poland first went to settle in America. He was only there a few days when he heard about gold in South Africa so he caught the ship; he landed at Cape Town and never went up to the Transvaal to look for gold. He made bread instead. His wife could not speak English, only Yiddish, and even though she could not write her name she was at the till of their bakery. They lived in Hanover Street, but when their house got too full with their children, two sons rented rooms near us. One son became a surgeon.

Often I had to take for Aunty Titus – she was the spinster lady who rented a room with my friend Irine's family – her unbaked bread to put in the Gordin's oven when their own bread was finished. They charged two pennies for a big loaf and half a penny for a small loaf.

There were bright pink and yellow cup cakes very tempting on the shelves at the bakery, so we sometimes ran with our baked bread when it was finished and instead of paying for the baking, we ran out the back door and came back into the shop and bought a cookie. I think the Gordins knew but they never said anything.

The two men who did the baking were Japan and Harry, they were good men, always laughing. Sometimes they gave us the stale cookies. When we went to buy suurdeeg from them – they kept this yeast in a big tin, it was always bubbling, and they ladled it in a mug for us, a penny a mug.

Other times I was sent to Mrs Blecher to buy portions of chicken, we also got eggs from her. Rosie would make soup for all of us out of pieces of chicken, we could never afford a whole one.

We improvised songs about Mrs Kaplan and Mrs Gordin.

Mr Friedman was the manager of the National bioscope. He knows everybody, even the skollies, but he doesn't want the skollies in the bioscope, so he often calls the police, but that is only the drunk skollies who force their way in and are rude to him.

'Hey, you vark,' the drunk skollies shout, but most greet him and even from Bloemhof flats they know him because they must pass the bioscope. Wherever they go they must pass: to church, to school, for some were teachers, or to Tennant Street, or to Hanover Street, and he nods to some, waves to some, talks to some, maybe about a film or something, and he knows everybody by name. Even the poor whites who came down from near the fire brigade. Everyday Mr Friedman stands outside that bioscope, greeting poeple and waiting for the Saturday matinée to start – Saturdays there were three shows, one at 2 o'clock, one at 5.30 p.m. and then at 8 p.m. Sometimes Mr Friedman clicks the tickets, but mostly he stands around.

I was barred once from going in.

We were playing ball in the street and a ball goes against his head, he had a big head with a bles kop, I don't know if I did it on purpose or what: 'You bloody bastard,' he shouts at me.

'You bastard yourself,' I say back.

'You not coming in here again – you barred,' he said.

I stayed away a long time, but slowly I go back again. Ruby takes me in so he can't bar me. She buys the ticket and takes my hand and I walk past Mr Friedman – he can't say a thing. 'Hello Mr Friedman,' Ruby says.

And now after all those years he lives in Sea Point in a flat and sometimes takes a walk and sees me as I get off the bus to walk to work: 'Hello,' he says, but I don't think he actually remembers me, but he must know I was once one of those who lived in District Six and went to the National.

5 School

We had a beautiful school at the corner of Tennant and William Streets, it was big and we had everything in it. I loved school.

I was in the Afrikaans class and Irine my close friend was in the English class, another friend, Shirley Matthews who lived next door, an English speaker, was one class higher.

For school I used to wear a white blouse and a navy gym and royal blue girdle. I used to run to school. I never ate because there wasn't time, but I took my sandwiches, thick, thick slices, in those days we never knew about thin slices.

When the boys behind used to pinch me then I'd screech aloud. Otherwise I was a little shy at school and if it was just my plaits they pulled I'd giggle.

We had coloured teachers and they stayed in Salt River. They'd pass our house when they went home, sometimes I'd be sitting in front of our house where we had a pergola and an old grapevine twisted around it, and I'd sit under it on a bench and they'd wave to me.

At the back of our house there was a big fir tree, and you had to climb a ladder to go to a higher level where Dadda made a lovely garden with lots of flowers. It was his garden and he doesn't want anyone in it. White lilies, big, big sunflowers, carnations. Down below we kept chickens and even turkeys once.

But I used to take a whole gang from school and we must be careful when we go and play up there because at night when Dadda comes home and waters his garden he sees footprints and he's wild.

I also took the gang in our diningroom where we had big glass doors with all those pretty blues and reds around it, the glass shone with its reflections in the afternoon sun. We used to sit there looking at the colours.

Sometimes children bunked school – I didn't because I loved school, but once my Dadda thought I bunked because he came home at lunch time and found me home. My teacher had sent me home because I was sick with whooping cough. Dadda just hit me: 'Why didn't you go to school? You onbeskof.' He didn't give me a chance to explain. Okkie was home and told him I was sent home, he still

didn't believe that, perhaps I didn't look sick, but later he heard me whoop.

Dadda chased my brother Okkie for bunking school, but Okkie ran onto our roof; Dadda caught him later and took him to school, but he bunked again and Dadda hit him hard. Then Okkie just wouldn't go back. Then it was only me at school.

I loved Thursdays.

Every Thursday we had one hour proper school and then we went to Father Hudson of St Marks and had a proper church service with choir boys. The church was full and we had holy communion with bread and wine and sat confessions. We sang hymns and had full mass. The church is still there, big and old, with nothing round it.

Singing was my best.

In Standard Four we had singing with a teacher from England with a big red face, she was a big woman and very strict, she was pushing us. We had to sing over and over one song.

Then our school and nine others were to sing in a festival at the City Hall. Each school sang one song, but then all ten schools went on that stage to sing a song: each school had one part and at the end we sang together.

No one from my house would go to the City Hall and watch the concert, so I was not going, how could I with no one to take me? Then a school friend – not one I bring home, she lives higher up and she fetches me sometimes in the morning because she passes our house – Anita told her mother they must take me to the City Hall.

That afternoon when I get home from school so happy, Rosie washed and ironed my uniform – because she doesn't move out of our house, she does everything, and cleans my shoes; I had saved them and not worn them for a month.

So that night no one was interested from my house, Dadda went to sleep, but all the other children, their mothers and sisters and fathers and aunties went. It was house full.

Cilla the bitch she could have taken me.

Dadda used to come home sometimes at lunch times to give my sister Rosie money so she could buy meat or bread or potatoes if she needed it, and he could tell her what food to make for supper and check up on things. So twice a day he could check up, and the sjambok would come out even at lunch times if we needed it. But I didn't hate my father, he was a good strict father who cared, and that is how it should be.

And that is what I tell my children now, they should have had such a father, and they should have lived in District Six with so many relatives and friends ready to split on you and keep an eye on you, they watched you and checked up on you, you couldn't get away with nothing.

That is why I always went to school with my legs black and blue.

At nine o'clock every night Rosie would be finished in the kitchen, everything was cleared, the boys had washed up, Dadda was in bed, and I was lying in bed too, reading a book.

Then Leonard and Rosie would begin to sing in the kitchen. It's cold outside, winter, and the two of them sit in front of the coal stove while it's still hot and sing there. Songs like, 'There's a home without a mother,' or 'White Christmas' and other Bing Crosby songs and favourites from the coons.

I lay in bed and listened, sometimes I could not stand it any more and I'd put my book down and I'd go and join them, then slowly we'd all get out of bed and sing and sing.

6 Friends

Lizzie is calling me: 'Come Hettie, run, the coons are on their way to Rosebank.'

I was so excited, Lizzie chose me from all her friends in the street. I was busy playing with my 'poor toys', ones that Okkie made for me, this one was a tin with wire strung through that I sometimes pulled and sometimes pushed. I dropped it and followed Lizzie.

It was hot and far to walk, but I didn't complain. 'Come on Hettie,' she pulled me.

Lizzie was twelve and she belonged to the Dronkies – they were the people who lived close to us off another lane, there were six single rooms and families in each, they always played in the street, those children, and none of them cared; their houses were dirty and I loved it. In Lizzie's house there were ten of them, all just running around and often not bothering to go to school.

I loved Lizzie and her family, Lizzie was clever.

We started dancing after the coons until we got to Rosebank, then Lizzie looked in through big gates and whoops! she was gone. I stand and look around, I call: 'Lizzie, Lizzie,' but in that crowd she has vanished. I must stay at that gate and not move away, Lizzie will come back to find me. I get so tired I sit down. I am scared stiff. I don't know how many hours I sit there, but the people start coming out, the coons dancing and singing their way past me, and then some stragglers come out.

I am tired and frightened and I begin to cry. I know it's late because the sun is going down behind the mountain, it must be six o'clock.

'Haai, hier's mos Magpie's suster,' Magpie was my brother Stan's nickname. I looked up and saw three or four boys, I knew them, they were Stan's friends, from the Hungry Hill gang, the boys who used to hang around on the corners smoking, singing, good little skollies. 'Lizzie's gone, I'm lost,' I cry.

'Kom, ons gaan jou huistoe vat.'

'We're taking you to your pa.'

When I heard this I was frightened, but I was so tired that I don't know how I walked to the station; they paid my ticket, then we still had to walk home. 'Don't go to the house with me.'

'Yes, we are taking you to your pa.'

'My pa is sleeping.'

'We'll wake him up and tell him we found you in Rosebank.'

They took me in and Dadda got up on a chair and got down a leather strap which was hooked high up. I ran to the toilet.

'Come out,' Dadda shouted.

'I'm peeing.'

Dadda waited. It was raining, it was so unusual, a summer rain. I had to go out, I could not sit there so cold now.

Dadda started hitting. 'Jy gaan nie weer met daardie kinders van die dronkies nie.'

But Lizzie was always laughing, always running, running after men and happy-go-lucky. With my mother dead and no one really to see what I did after school, when I was free I was with Lizzie.

Once Lizzie and I took chickens to be slaughtered for the Gordins. It was the end of the Sabbath and the Jewish people wanted chicken for their Sunday lunch.

There was a yard next to the house and in the yard two big drums filled with cement; a plank was across them and on the plank big nails. Mr Shapiro would take the chicken, tie the feet together, hold the wings then quickly cut the chicken's throat and let the blood drip out.

The light from their diningroom shone through the window and on to the chickens and that yard, and there were feathers everywhere, and all the people waiting for their fowls to be 'koshered'.

If I could paint, I would paint that picture, of the Saturday night at the slaughterer with all the mess, the blood and the feathers, and then they would give us a tickey if we would hose down the yard. I often think: The Shapiro family's son could study and become a doctor just from them killing chickens.

One of my other special friends was Noreen. She and all of us – a whole gang of us – would go and play where the trees grew at De Waal Drive. We called it our 'green curtains'. And when it was hot summer days we'd go and run through the trees, all of us, twelve or thirteen years old, and when we couldn't run any more we'd go and lie down on the grass.

Then Noreen and I would lie together. I say to Noreen: 'I want to be big and get out of the house and get married and not get hidings, and I only want one child, because I saw how sore it is with Ruby, she screams and screams when her babies come.'

'And I want lots of babies,' Noreen says, 'I don't think about a husband!'

7 Aunty Titus

I liked to go to Irine over the road and hear 'The Creaking Door' on their wireless. They were a big family, all working, I was glad we could listen to that programme together.

There was a spinster lady boarding with Irine's family: Aunty Titus, she rented a room upstairs.

She didn't like Irine, because Irine was a spoiled brat, and she was cheeky and rude to her granny who was Aunty Titus's age – I was the best one.

Sometimes I did her shopping. I liked to go into her room, she had all sorts of old things, like old pictures, and a little table with tea things all nicely put out. She had a kettle in her room and always made tea for me and gave me a biscuit or sweets. She gave me five pennies for doing her shopping and then I could go to bioscope – the bioscope was next door to that house.

She was not my real aunt, but just like one.

Irine always told me that the old woman upstairs from her wanted her to do her shopping, but she didn't want to do it. So one day I went and that old woman was so fond of me; I liked so much to go into her room and in the end I was touching on there nearly every day to see if she wanted anything done.

I didn't speak English, like the others in the house did, and Aunty Titus spoke Afrikaans. I was the only one who visited her – and sometimes one of her family's sons.

Her little room had an olden times clock, a bed, a dresser with ornaments on it, a wardrobe; and I was the only one who can come into that room, she calls me to have tea with her, and gives me what-ever she's got. Often she fries fish for me, stock fish or maasbanker I'd bought for her, on a double stove with wicks, she pours in para-ffin; or she fries me polony and egg. So every day after school I buy her half a bread or fish or whatever she needs, and she waits for me every afternoon, and I go straight to her.

Aunty Titus paid for half my school books.

She is a Christian, my mother was also friendly with her.

When we finish eating she washes my plate, gives me sweets and money, and then watches me from her stoep as I play in the street.

I will never forget the day she said to me: 'I hear they are going to move Irine's family from here, what will happen to me?'

She was frightened. She didn't talk much since she heard these things.

Ever since I can remember she had lived with that family, but even now she still did not like Irine to go into her room or sit on her bed because sometimes when I was with Aunty Titus, Irine would just come with me, then Aunty Titus would wait till Irine left; she had hidden her little hanky in her wardrobe and I must sit and wait as she undoes one knot and another knot and then out would come some money: 'That is for you, for the school concert,' then she would close the wardrobe again, 'I'm glad Irine is not here, she argues too much, she is not welcome here.'

And then one day she was very upset when I got to her after school. She was crying, she did not talk, so I went downstairs again to Irine.

Irine's family were all sitting together, then Irine said: 'Hettie, they are moving us to Bridgetown, we got the papers, they are going to break down this house. Bridgetown is so far Mommy says, and what will happen to her charring job?'

'And Aunty Titus? Where will she go?'

Irine said: 'I don't know Hettie, perhaps we will take her with us.'

I went up to Aunty Titus's bedroom the next afternoon and on the kitchen table was the prettiest cloth I had seen, all embroidered, and tea cups and saucers and plates laid out for two. Aunty Titus said: 'Go to Oubaas Pringle in Caledon Street' (that was the shop we could buy the cheapest from) 'and buy me some milk, sugar and that special Duens small bread, round on the top.'

When I come back she made me sit on the chair next to the table and she sat on the bed. She had made pudding, red jelly and custard. We sat together. I felt this was different from other days – that beautiful china, the cloth.

When we were finished eating she gave me some sweets and two little cookies.

'I'm going tomorrow Hettie – going to relatives I don't know, they live somewhere in Kensington.'

She looks so sad, she just sits. 'I am to be moved.'

Aunty Titus was very old then, she could hardly walk, I did not say goodbye to her, she could not have lived long in Kensington.

For a few weeks after that – because we were still in William Street then – I used to look up to that stoep just in case Aunty Titus would be standing there, watching me play.

And then the house was gone.

8 The sly one

Amina Simons and her husband Jacob lived next door to us in the lane, they shared the yard but we had our own toilets outside. Theirs was a single story house and smaller than ours; they had a dining-room, kitchen, two bedrooms and a hokkie in the back yard.

Their daughters were special friends of mine. Jacob had a horse and cart and he sold vegetables and fruit. He brought two boys from a farm who helped him, and they lived in that hokkie.

Jacob was a good man, a happy man, and he used to take us all for drives in the cart. We used to climb up and sit one on top of each other and drive up and down William Street, into Hanover Street, squashed in, shouting to friends and waving to Mrs Kaplan or Mrs Blecher cutting up the chickens, and sometimes old Mr Gordin would stop us and give us each a bright cookie.

We loved Prins the horse and Okkie decorated him with all Dadda's medals.

The two boys from the farm, they were brothers, Boesman and Lucky, were friendly with my brothers.

Then one day Amina's husband died. He just got sick and died, we didn't even know the poor man died.

But she, Amina, was such a bitch we couldn't even go into her house. She washed her husband's body herself, so stingy, we just saw people fetch the body, no funeral.

Amina, that stingy one, just stayed in her house with everything closed up, the windows, the doors, we never went in there, we just played outside. Noreen was my special friend, but of course we were all friendly.

Amina sewed herself and made nice clothes for her daughters, and she saw that the girls' hair was always nicely combed with ribbons and all, but she wouldn't sew for anyone else. Not like my mother used to be, or other women in District Six, they'd help; she could have told my father, 'Just buy the material and I'll make for Hettie also,' but she didn't, she was too stingy.

But her children didn't have the freedom we had, they stayed in the yard, they didn't go to bioscope and parties, the only time they were happy was when we played in the yard with them.

Those girls were not allowed to put on their new dresses straight away like we were, they only put them on for special occasions.

And then the sly one began to jol with the priest. He had a wife and stayed in Grassy Park and he came and visited her. Then Noreen, my friend, saw them sleeping together, so then he stayed away.

Then another man from higher up, a couple of streets away, he was also married, I think the two of them worked together, because she began to work.

She was a pretty woman then, well-built; she was a Malay turned Christian, but all her men were very skinny, Jacob her husband was skinny, the priest was skinny and this new one also. The men were all scared of her, Amina was bossy.

So this man was visiting her now and the whole street knows. Night time he comes and brings things, chocolates and fruit for the children, little parcels with luxuries, but the door stays closed, and the windows, and the affair gets bigger, and we are never allowed inside that stingy one's house.

Then the Group Areas come and they moved to Bloemhof Flats where everyone would have loved to move, and that is before any of us have got our areas where to go. There was much talk of how she got that flat. How did she get in there? We didn't know, but we guessed. She must have had other affairs. It was impossible to get a flat there. Who wanted to be sent out of town to strange places?

Sammy used to see this latest one going to Amina: 'Haai, wat soek hy met haar?' he used to say. It was on everybody's mind that she was jolling, and she didn't talk to anyone in the street, just walked with her head in the air. There was something odd.

In Bloemhof flats the second man started coming again, and after she finished that one off – he died – she gets busy with the priest again, everyone said she was a hard woman.

Then her girls got married in Bloemhof flats. Posh people stay in Bloemhof flats, school teachers, principals; they all talk English there.

But Amina had no heart, look what she did to her own sister who came to her when her husband was out of work. She told her sister to wash her children outside under the cold tap, the children were crying, and all of us in William Street spoke about it.

And Bloemhof flats is still in District Six, but it's for whites. Police stay there and they restored the flats. All Boers live there now.

So Amina had to be moved again, even she didn't have enough sway with the Group Areas people to remain there. They moved to Lavendar Hill, the ugliest place, they give it to the coloureds.

And then one day I saw her son-in-law and he told me that Amina is now married to the priest and they live in Lavendar Hill together, his wife died.

Noreen I saw years later. She lives in Bonteheuwel. Her dreams did not come true, how we used to dream up there under the trees, our green curtains. It didn't help that she lived with posh people and wanted a big family. She has one child and her sister lives in Bishop Lavis – they are all lonely and struggling.

And the two boys who lived in the hokkie in their yard, Boesman and Lucky, Amina didn't want them sleeping in the yard when her husband died, so they moved away, they went to stay with the Malays over the road. But the Malays got used to them, they were good boys, but so bloody ugly.

They always used to be so good to my father, when he was sick they'd hold him and help him up the street.

Boesman was a friend of my brother Kevin, they went to Valkenberg together, they both had breakdowns. But I think it was the dagga, they were acting mad.

My Dadda was glad they sent my brother away. He stayed at Valkenberg for three months, but he never smoked dagga again. My Dadda said it was good, they fixed him there.

Those Malays who took the two brothers were well off, their whole family stayed in that street. Hadji Cassiem took the boys plus he had a lot of children himself.

The boys helped his wife with the children, they carried them. Every year the wife got another baby, and that baby grows, and then just seeing Boesman and Lucky they get very fond of them and the two boys stayed with the Malays a long time, becoming part of the family; Hadji Cassiem protected the boys, sometimes they got wild and he gets them out of jail and was a father to them.

They disappeared with the Group Areas, I never saw them again. Everyone just went their way.

9 Escaping

Upstairs we had a lodger, Issie Karstens, he rented a room for him and his three, sons, Leo, Jeffrey and Cecil. Their mother died before I was born.

That man was a joller, he goes out every night and comes home in the morning. Then he got married again and the stepmother was cheeky to the boys, and she complains about them when Issie comes home. Their room was on top of mine. I hear the boys screaming when the father comes home and he is hitting the hell out of them all. They had no one to stand up for them.

Sammy talked to the father.

Then the father died, he was the one who fell off the stretcher, and the stepmother was alone with them and she was not interested in them and she left. One was my age, his name was Leo.

One day Leo asked me for a date. I said: 'Ja.' And then I got so scared because his eyes look at me as if he's not normal. So I didn't turn up for the date at the time I should have met him, I stayed inside.

Then Ruby went out to the street at twelve o'clock – it was a hot night. She went to call her two sons, and then Leo saw her and he must have been full of dagga, and in his mind it must have been that Ruby was keeping me inside. So he thought Ruby knows about our date, and he's chopping away on a pole with an axe. Ruby was calling her sons, and then he chopped Ruby's nose as he swung the axe. He sommer hit her like that.

All the neighbours came running and they called for an ambulance. I thought her whole nose was off, its lucky she's got a flat nose, I sometimes look at her nose now – and she just said: 'Leo hit me on the nose.'

I was laying in bed that night and I heard him chopping on the pole and thought: God he's chopping, God I'm not going outside. Then I heard screaming, and everyone ran, and I felt such a fool I said nothing to anyone about the date, I just kept quiet.

Ruby never could understand why Leo hit her with the chopper.

Leo always had an eye for me and I wasn't interested because we grew up together so why must I be interested?

He went to jail after that: 'Leo het Ruby met die byl gekap, nou sit hy in tronk.' Everyone in William Street knew.

That night our house was full because Ruby's got such a big voice, she screamed. I was shaking in my boots, I'm not going to stick my head outside for a whole month. I stayed inside. You can still see the mark on Ruby's nose, if she had a high nose like me he would have chopped it in half.

If Ruby wasn't there, I don't know what would have happened to me because then I think I would have got that chopper.

Leo was terrible. I still played with the other boys, running in the street, but I never would go out with them. In any case, I still went to school.

My sister Cilla's best friend was also Cilla – and that Cilla had two sons named William and Eddie, they lived four houses up in William Street.

We had a gramophone you wind up, it was in the boys' room and we played lovely records, Bing Crosby, and hymns, and always there were people coming to listen and sing, that room was always full. William and Eddie were regulars, they were about my age.

When Group Areas came in, Cilla, who was very white, her father was from England, looked at the white areas to live and I can't say how but she did go and live up in Devil's Peak in a white area.

She lived like a white and her sons grew up as whites, but you wouldn't say Cilla had coloured blood in her.

We didn't hear from them again once they left William Street, perhaps they were frightened. I think William and Eddie must have missed the street and all their friends; they went to white schools now.

And then we read in the papers about a murder, and it was William who committed that murder. He turned ducktail, a dagga rooker, long hair, and in the photo in the paper he looked dirty – that was the ducktail time – though he always used to be clean.

He murdered a schoolgirl in Vredehoek, and he hanged for that murder.

When I think of the happy days when they were running in and out of our house, I wonder what happened.

10 Ruby

None of my brothers had ever brought girls to the house. Then Sammy brought a girl, we never knew they had got married. She came, and she stayed for good; that was the day Sammy brought Ruby.

My father didn't like Ruby, she was too black: 'You bring a swart vrou, kyk die lippe!'

I can never understand Dadda about that, but then much later he said the Indian boy I was seeing was too dark, he liked blondes, and I suppose just as some people like redheads or gingers, it was simply a preference. Or maybe be already knew the dangers of being too dark in our country: he may have sensed extra trouble for us.

Ruby tried to be good, but nothing she said or did could get past him, but Mother could see Ruby would be a good wife for Sammy.

Dadda was cross with Sammy, but he built them a hokkie in our back yard. There were chickens and ducks and tortoises roaming around in the yard. In a little corner of the hokkie was the kitchen, with a primus stove, and in winter it was nice and warm; there was a double bed and a wardrobe.

Sammy never had friends, he was just with his little dark Ruby, and every year a baby came. They looked all right when they are small, but when they were three they turned out with big lips like Ruby.

Ruby looked so black, but she was coloured.

I used to play with the children, but I could only go when Dadda was not home; I mustn't go there because they are too black.

Ruby was all right to us, we liked her better than our own sisters, and as time went on, she meant more and more to me.

Ruby worked hard, she scrubbed the yard and cleaned the holes around the yard, she was scared of germs. Ruby had four children in that hokkie.

Every year Sammy used to say: 'Mamma gaan weer a baby kry,' he was so shy when he said it.

And Ruby used to make a hell of a noise when she gave birth to her babies, she screamed so the whole street can hear her, and made funny sounds like Mmmmmmm; she makes that noise for two days before the baby comes. Ruby screams the roof down, and the whole street comes to see. She has all her babies at home.

The Malay woman from over the road and my sister Rosie clean the room; the midwife comes from the Peninsula Hospital, or sometimes two nurses come. Afterwards the Malay woman helps clean the baby, and washes up the room and the nappies. We all help each other.

The whole street stands around and waits to see if it is a girl or boy when it's finished.

Ruby has big babies, eight or nine pounds, and she wears big, big dresses when she's pregnant, she gets like an elephant, her feet swell up, she can hardly walk. She was a good woman.

So there among the geese that chased us, the chickens running free, and us throwing tops and ball, was Ruby in her hokkie. I loved that hokkie.

Every day Sammy had to walk down the passage of our house right through the house, through the kitchen and out the kitchen door into the back yard to get to his hokkie, and always past Dadda.

Ruby used to cook beautifully in her little corner. Sweet-sour curries, maasbankers, silver fish – she used to go to the docks and bring us fish.

Ruby used to take me to the docks with her when she went to see her brother Cliff. He was on a fishing trawler. The two of us, we used to go to the penny ferry and go over the water to get to the trawler, it was nice if it was a fine day. We would find Cliff sitting outside the trawler doing work, getting ready for the next trip. Cliff always gave us money to get back again.

Cliff was at sea most of his life, he had polio when he was a child and was crippled in one leg.

When Cliff returned from trawling and was on leave, he would stay in the hokkie with Ruby and Sammy, and his friends would visit and bring us snoek, tuna heads, big, big heads, and soles, and all kinds of fish. Ruby would start dishing out fish for all the neighbours.

Ruby kept Cliff's guitar in the hokkie tied up in the one corner, and when four or five of Cliff's friends from the trawler came, all drunk, full of money, they would start making food, smoking fish, singing with that guitar – all in that hokkie.

Cliff was also in the coons every year when he took his leave, he could keep up with the coons even with his stiff leg, he was very short and very popular. 'Hello Cliff, hello Cliff,' as he walks past with the coons; he waves and he walks.

48

We children always knew when Cliff was at our house. We just saw smoke hanging in the air, he was smoking fish with lots of cayenne pepper on the snoek.

Sometimes Cliff stayed for a week and it was Monday nights fish night, Tuesday night pumpkin stew, Wednesday penny polony night. We bought that polony from the Jewish butcher, it was a meaty sausage and it was boiled or stewed with potatoes; it was my favourite supper – when I went to fetch that polony they always gave me a tiny sausage to eat on my way home.

Ruby always took me with her, once a year, when we all went on a picnic. We went in a big lorry, all the neighbours, all Ruby's children, and Dadda doesn't even know I'm going, he only discovers it when he checks up at midnight, and then my sister Cilla talks to him and he forgets. Cilla looks the most like my mother.

All people, old, young, went with Ruby, she gets this lorry and Ruby takes her doppie brandy, all her brothers come with and they all drunk from the docks with other fishermen too. We go to Oudekraal and we leave District Six in the middle of the night and get there in the middle of the night. Then we start putting up our tents.

Each house gets its tent. We all bring food, make big fires, they drink, sing around the fire, and there are always babies, nine or ten of them.

Gadidja has brought her drum, and then she plays.

We swim the next day and make fires again and eat and sing. Late in the afternoon it's time to go home. Finally we are all piled in the lorry again, and now Gadidja plays the drum.

All over District Six they hear us coming back and every house comes out to shout hello.

11 Rumours

One day Sammy took Ruby for a walk through the gardens in the avenue.

A policeman stopped them: 'Hey, what are you doing with a white man?' he asked Ruby.

'He's my husband,' Ruby whispers, she is so frightened.

'Stop it, I'm warning you – what is your name?

A coloured policeman who was also walking there recognised Sammy and came to tell the white one.

But the white policeman said again: 'Jy moet met die darkies gaan, nie die Whities,' then he turned to the coloured policeman and said: 'Wat loop die wit man met die kaffir?'

Sammy said to the policeman who knew him: 'Sê ek is bruin.'

He did. Lucky that man knew Sammy, otherwise he would have gone to jail.

Sammy never took Ruby for a walk again.

He told our father about the talk he heard where he worked, there at the supreme court, that they were going to throw us out of District Six.

Dadda did not want to talk about it, and never about apartheid. Dadda is silent, not saying what he is thinking.

Then one day Sammy comes home and again he said: 'Dadda, I live in a hokkie, but I love it, I made this little kitchen, and Dadda they are going to come and chuck us out. I am telling you it is all the talk.'

Dadda looked up and Sammy was crying.

'Yes, the Malays opposite saw inspectors looking around. Sammy, what do you think they are doing?'

It was the first time Dadda would speak about it. I was very frightened. My sister used to say it was rumours.

'They are going to throw us out, I don't know where,' Sammy said.

'Where are they going to take us?' Dadda asked.

'I don't know Dadda.'

Rosie joined in. It was strange whenever there was something important to say it always took place in the front room, the girls' bedroom, we didn't have a lounge so usually we sat in the kitchen. I was

lying in the big double bed rolled up like a cocoon. I held my breath and listened.

'Are they going to separate us?' Rosie asked. She had a boyfriend over the road, a Malay.

A few days later we heard a terrible commotion and crying from the Malay house over the road. Mrs Fakir was calling for Sammy because she knew he worked at the supreme court and thought he could help her. The inspector had been and had a little book and said their house had to be evacuated.

They were the first people in our road to get papers. They just sent them a letter to say they must come to the city council and they will be told where they were to be moved.

Of course Sammy could do nothing.

'Waar gaan hulle nou vir ons sit?' Mrs Fakir asked Sammy.

Sammy did not know.

'And now this place will be going for the whites?' Mrs Fakir asked.

Everyone in the room was asking: 'We must move out to make room for whites?'

Such was the talk all over District Six – and I didn't realise it would be so quick to get rid of us.

Until apartheid Dadda kept us all together, and then it was lucky he died before we were forced away.

I often think it was his fear of what they will do to us the darker our skins were that made him so frightened of black skins.

Dadda always used to say: 'One day the Russians will come and take South Africa.'

Dadda got a stroke and died.

12 Moving

Inspectors from the council came and took photos of all the houses, then they wrote down things in a book.

They came to us: 'Who all is staying in this house? How many in a family?'

'We have two families in this house,' Sammy answered while Rosie stood by.

The people in District Six were all talking among each other, they had a feeling they were going to be moved.

The Group Areas office is in Burg Street, we have to go there and fill in papers and they start asking you questions again, who is in the family and all that. Then you wait till they allot you something. They divide the families up.

When you get a house you pay in advance.

Gadidja was one of the first to be moved. They were like a family to us. Sammy seeing all the old people who watched him grow up now leaving, they all people who know us so well from Gadidja's house – Sammy who was born there, like all of us, he never stopped crying.

After our street was emptied, they started knocking all the houses down with bulldozers.

It was a shock when we had to move, as with all the people there. How were we going to continue to work?

By this time I was working now for a madam in Sea Point, but I could go home every night. District Six was my refuge – a place to feel safe and happy, it was wonderful to come home at night and be with all my people. Now we were going far out to places we never heard of before. Our family broke up:

Sammy and Ruby and family to Netreg.

Myself and Rosie and our families, Sammy and Ruby took us in.

Lenny – to Belhar.

Cilla – to Belhar. She took Lenny because she could not leave him without a place, where could he go?

Albert – he was at sea at that time.

Kevin and his wife Ellen – Elsies River.

Stan – he was a painter, to Heideveld.

Okkie – he worked in Spar, he married and went to Bishop Lavis.

Tommy – he also went with Cilla, and later when Stan died he moved in with Ellen.

For months we had it hanging over our heads we would have to move.

As the men looked around our house and in the street and wrote things, we wondered: 'What is going on?' At that stage we were not told anything definite.

It got into the papers. District Six frozen – going for whites. District Six a white area!

The old people could not take it, it was the only home they knew, they'd never been out of District Six. Lots of them died.

Sammy cried so much when he left.

Ruby said to me: 'Wait for me here in town. I will come back and fetch you and Rosie.'

It was a Saturday morning. It can't be happening, I thought, I wish I could get my bed back and we didn't have to be going.

I looked around, I didn't see curtains up in our house, everything empty, empty. My sister had packed everything up, like our clothes. I was so afraid of where I was going, and with Sarah, my daughter, so far from town.

I had watched others going, and now it was my turn. The shock was on us all.

Sammy used to go to William Street every Saturday for some time, that was when all was empty but not knocked down yet, and he just sat there and looked and cried. Slowly, slowly, everyone went, and Cape Town died.

One day Sammy was sitting there and a policeman came to him: 'Hey, Whitey, get away, the bulldozer is coming.'

'I'm coloured. I'm going to Netreg, sir, I live there now, I'm just looking sir.'

'Oh, you are an ordentlike kleurling,' the policeman said and walked away.

Sammy told us how Mrs Ofsowitz – 'My Lady' we called her, she spoke and acted just like one of us, she wore takkies and long dirty dresses and could she swear! – she too had to get out. And she was white; she also cried so much.

One by one people got their places.

The Society Ones became school teachers and they had money and bought a place in Athlone.

There was no choice, you got your notice, you went where they put you.

To me it seemed the government controlled every movement, they could do just what they wanted with our lives.

When Sammy and Ruby went, Sammy's last words were: 'It was such a nice place for our children – playing ball in the streets, the bioscope just there, the fish market, everything was near, you could just walk.'

And all he'd had was a hokkie.

Sammy was so miserable in Netreg, he loves gardening and outside his hokkie he used to grow so many plants and love them all. He tries here in Netreg, there's a patch of sand, but his heart is not in it.

Sammy does not mix with anyone here. Ruby stays at home too, Ruby who used to love people so much, and go down to the docks and to the markets, she can't take the long walk to the station so she goes nowhere.

All Ruby's daughters are enormous, fat, they all have skinny husbands. And sometimes when Ruby's brother comes and he gets a dop in him, it's not like he was in District Six, happy and laughing, now he wants to fight, and now Sammy also wants to fight and he says to Ruby: 'Your children are blacks.'

He and Ruby argue: 'En jou broer, wat soek die kaffir hier?' It's like he is blaming Ruby for everything, I can't believe it, he loved Ruby so much.

And as every Christmas and New Year comes, Sammy just cries, he gets so heartsore, he thinks of our mother and the days in District Six.

Ruby did try to char for a while but it was too far, I think she is not healthy any more. To visit anyone even just the other side of Netreg you must take a bus or taxi and that is money.

I still dream of that house in William Street.

13 Siesie

In the Malays, if you are the eldest, they call you Siesie. Siesie lived in William Street lower down, she worked as a cleaner in Woolworths, in town.

That Malay family all stayed together not too far from the bioscope and the Indian shop. They were a big family.

Siesie married an African, he worked as a waiter in a hotel, he was a good husband, smiling, a nice man, we all knew him well and liked him.

So they lived with her mother and though he was from Transkei he had all the coloured ways, he knew nothing else, he grew up with us. I don't know how that happened.

They had seven children.

In 1967 when everyone was moving, one by one we were getting a letter, Siesie was with her mother all the time, and then the senior inspectors came and asked who stays here, how many children are married – and then they discovered Siesie is married to an African, so they gave her a house in Langa.

'If you don't move there with your children we will deport your husband, he will be sent back to Transkei,' they tell Siesie. But that man never knew the Transkei, he was a baby in Cape Town.

'You cannot stay in a coloured area,' that is what they tell Siesie.

So Siesie and her husband and the children went to Langa. They took their furniture, and all the children. She had to travel to Cape Town to her work, like her husband.

She came to visit her mother in William Street, she was the woman who was so good and did so many errands for everyone, shopping for them and if something goes cheap at the market she buys it for her neighbours.

'Mama,' Siesie is crying, 'I can't take it there, there is only a communal toilet, we are not used to that Mama. The children don't know anyone and their ways are different. I can't take it.' Siesie broke down.

Siesie went back, there was nothing she could do. But three months later she packed her children up and she and her husband came back to her mother in William Street. She could not take it any more in Langa, she said it was like a desert there.

But the authorities found out and they said they were sending her husband away. Then she begged them to allocate her a house in a coloured area, and later she got a house in Steenberg. Meanwhile her husband remained in Langa, the plan was that secretly he would join her whenever he could. They took his house away from him in Langa because he was now a man on his own, and gave him a room.

Siesie got a house but the authorities found out about her husband not staying in Langa and they deported him to Transkei.

Her mother, that kind woman, still running around for people, could do nothing for her own daughter Siesie. If there was an accident her mother would give first aid and she did nursing if people were sick; she was a Malay, but she helped Christians, making a pot of soup, baking cakes; she gave plates of food even though they were poor themselves. Every sick person knew she would help them. When the Malays used to fast, long ago before the Group Areas split us up, it was she who would give everyone cakes when they broke their fast.

So now Siesie and her man, who had all those children and had been married seventeen years, were separated forever.

Siesie's twin girls were brought up like real Malays, always clean and dressed in lovely clothes. They lived in Retreat and Siesie worked hard because now there was no money coming from her husband, and he had earned good money.

Siesie's twins could not take it and missed their father so much and went to look for him in the Transkei. They got a lift, but that family had such bad luck. Going there the car went over a cliff as they went through a pass and they were killed. The man who drove the car was concussed and it took him three days to climb up the pass and report the accident. He still has nightmares hearing Siesie's daughters' screams.

Siesie was expecting her daughters back on the Friday to start work again. When they did not return on Saturday she has a feeling something has happened. Then she got the telegram.

Siesie got diabetes from the shock. They had been such a happy family. She is dead now, and she never saw her husband again, nor did he see his children or his wife again. Such a quiet man, he didn't fight, never argued, a proper gentleman, everyone in the street loved him.

He was never allowed back, I don't know what happened to him. Good, hardworking people. A whole family destroyed.

14 I become a mother

I fell pregnant, the father was an Indian. I had my daughter Sarah, and I stayed at home with Dadda. My sisters helped me look after Sarah, but Ruby was the real one to help me.

I started to work, got a job in Sea Point. The madam had small children and I worked long hours. The children loved me, I made them laugh, I told them all about what I do when I get home, what it's like in the streets there and about the coons. I taught them lots of the songs, and the dances. They always wanted to visit my house, they even wanted to come and stay with me.

I cooked – I had learned because by now I had helped in the house – and I cooked Malay cooking and Indian cooking, and now I learned Jewish cooking. My madam said I had a real taste for food, I could season food better than anyone she knew.

We had lots of fights at first, but now that we are both older the madam tells me her nerves were bad with all that was happening in the country and thinking she is white and bringing up her children in a society she didn't like – so we had our fights, but we have stayed together.

In those days I used to go home every night because I only had to catch one bus, and at night my whole family was together and I saw my friends. But my Indian boyfriend stopped paying me maintainance which was four rands a month. I went to court and they made him pay me more, and then he disappeared. Perhaps he went back to India.

It was then that Sammy who worked at the supreme court heard the people talk while he was cleaning, and came home with more and more stories, and looked so worried. 'Dadda, you can't even vote any more – remember all the excitement on voting days? And still you won't listen to me – you don't want to talk apartheid and us being chucked out!'

'What can I do?'

And when I leave Sea Point at night and go home when I've finished my work, I look up at all those flats, some with just one rich woman living alone in a big flat – I know because I have gone to help make tea when they have bridge afternoons – I think: Gee, such

beautiful flats and so lonely. They sit on the phone and invite people
... and here in District Six when I get home it's crowded full of
noises, full of people, full of friends. And a happiness comes over
me, and I think, I don't want to be rich, to be rich is to be lonely.

Life was so easy in William Street – and now it seem as though the
Group Areas is going to take all the joy away – it's as if something is
sliding away from me.

So Ruby met me and Sarah and my sister Rosie on Saturday morning
at the Parade and we all went, with our carriers full of our things, to
the station, on our way to stay with Ruby and Sammy in Netreg.

I left those friends who were still in District Six, most likely never
to see them again.

It was while I was working for the madam in Sea Point that our
family was split up. Now I had to go all the way to Netreg instead of
just to William Street.

I'm glad my father died then. It was lucky too that my mother died
before apartheid, who knows, maybe they would have told my
mother to leave my father because she looked so white?

Madam and I laugh when I say this.

I used to take Sarah to work sometimes because she was just the
same age as my madam's little girl. But a neighbour objected and I
heard her say to Sarah: 'What are you doing here in Sea Point? You cannot play with white children.' Her little girl also used to come and play.

Then Sarah began to stutter.

When I came to work I used to hide her. I used to catch a very early
train and bus so that no one would see Sarah, and then disappear
when it was dark. I used to give her supper because then I could just
put her straight to bed when I got home. But Madam didn't want
trouble with the neighbours and besides it was the law.

One day that neighbour saw me in the street and said: 'You are not
allowed to bring your child here.' I could not understand her, she
used to leave sandwiches for the milk man, she seemed so good and
yet she could be cruel. 'I won't bring Sarah again, I don't want her to
be insulted,' I said to Madam.

When we were first told we had to leave our house in William
Street I thought: 'Perhaps Madam who is white can help us –
perhaps we won't have to move out.'

But just as the people in our street thought that Sammy working
at the supreme court could help them but he couldn't even manage
to help us, so Madam could do nothing.

I will never forget Madam's face when she took me home to Will-iam Street not long before we left. Already most of the houses were empty and no one waved to her, and they looked at me suspiciously – like why I am in a posh white's car. Madam just said: 'Hettie, I tried, I went as high as I possibly could, the interviews I had chilled me to the bone. I don't understand, the Christian religion is based on love – love your neighbour, even love your enemy – they are breaking the strongest of the commandments.'

15 Mitchells Plain

And then one day I myself got allotted a house. By now I had Sarah and two boys, Matthew and Luke.

My house was to be in Mitchells Plain. I had no money and I had to pay R29 in advance, plus rental of R55 a month, so I borrowed from Madam.

It was Sarah and me that went and got furniture from the shops and had to pay that off. Sarah was working at a clothing factory. They wanted to know where I worked and phoned Madam and asked her a lot of questions; she gets very cross with those furniture people, they charge so much, but what could we do? So I bought a big divan and a double-decker bed because the rooms are small. Madam said I must get a fridge because I can keep proper milk.

And I thought it would be nice to make jelly and keep ice-cream. I bought a second-hand hot plate, and a kettle, and I was given quite a lot of things, like blankets.

The house is far from town and the fares are very expensive, and because I must now take two jobs to pay everything off I get home very late and I am often frightened. I help Madam's daughter-in-law these days too.

I see skollies on the trains, but they are different from the skollies in District Six. In District Six we had decent skollies and I was not frightened of them. There I could walk in the streets in the middle of the night and not be touched.

They had gangs there, the Globe Gang, the Starlucks, the Killer Gang, The Mongrels, The Hungry Hills, and even a Junior Globe Gang. They never harmed you if you minded your own business. The leader of the Globe Gang, he had teeth full of gold, he was smart and suave and you'd never think he's a gangster. Even the tattooed ones from The Killer Gang who had skull and cross bones tattooed on them – bad buggers, people used to say – I was not even scared of them.

And now here a man got on at Bonteheuwel, his wife sat down next to me, she looked a decent woman with wedding rings on, and they talk, he's standing in front of me, there's no place for him to sit. Then I see all the tattoos on his face, on his lips, his ears and on his

hands – he is too ugly to look at – I think his whole body is full of tattoos, I bet his balls and all is covered in tattoos and I don't know how she can get in bed with him.

He looks like a long-time prisoner and he says to his wife: 'I've been away for a long time, three years, but I've got my unemployment card.' How anyone can give him work, I don't know, it makes you sick to look at him.

When I go to work in the morning, it's still dark when I leave, then the black guys get on the train and I must sit as they stand over me and beat on the back of my seat: Gooma, gooma, just like Gadidja's gooma, above my head, and my head goes doef, doef, from the sound and my nerves are not good. I don't move I am so frightened. I get such headaches every morning, bang, bang like that till we get to Cape Town. The train is crowded. There are no inspectors, no police, decent people sitting in the trains and we must take that.

Meanwhile the whites sit in comfort, they have their own trains with blinds, and they can read or lie back, but here I sit and the banging goes on and on, and on . . .

On Friday nights they start drinking on the trains and from Langa they walk up and down and swear and steal and when the train stops and there are electric failures – they often have black-outs, and the lights are off for two or three stations as the train moves on – you sit in the dark, you are scared of knives because everyone is standing with a knife out protecting themselves. And then you still have to get home and it is dangerous to go home.

I am sitting in the train and a priest is there: 'Have you got trouble at home? You look so sad, I see trouble on your face. There is a God that can help you, we can ask together, I can pray for you . . .'

His face comes closer as he talks about God and I'm glad when the train moves in to Cape Town station because of his breath, he was smelling like he didn't rinse his mouth from the night before.

'Your face looks troubled,' says a black woman another morning, she comes over to me from where she sat on the other corner, she talks to me in English. 'Something is wrong, something is worrying you.'

'No.'

I get kindness from an African woman.

16 Trouble

So I'm in my new house. I start a garden, I love gardening and flowers are my passion. I always think of Sammy's lovely garden with carnations and sweet peas, and my Dadda and his flowers, and now in this sandy soil I will see what I can grow. I take slips from Madam's garden and all her friends give me seeds and plants.

Sarah is staying with me, she has twins, but her husband lives with his mother so he can be nearer his work, he comes here at weekends. My two sons, Matthew is on a trawler and Luke works in a clothing factory, they are both in their twenties. Their father is a waiter at a hotel, but he still lives at home with his parents, he has to help them and his sisters.

I keep to myself here. I know no one. There isn't time anyway: I leave early to go to work, come home when it is dark. Then I cook, see to the children and grandchildren.

Weekends I clean the house properly, garden, do the washing and what a load of washing there is. I am lucky if I get any rest.

The neighbours across the road are very religious and they are preaching over the loudspeakers every night and have meetings all weekends.

One day they shout to Sarah. 'Why don't you pray with us, you don't go to church anyway.' And then they condemn the Catholic church and said we must pray with their group. Sarah said they must leave us alone. Meantime the noise all night was driving me mad but I said nothing.

Sarah's twins are playing in the garden and the woman comes out and she cursed them, swearing. Sarah went out and shouted back.

This is the first time I had witnessed division amongst us coloureds, especially over religion, and Sarah being so on her nerves.

Then eight of them came to our house that night and threw a broom at Sarah. She shouted and Matthew came out and smacked one of the men in his face. Someone called the police, they came and said we must sort it out ourselves.

How I went to work the next day I don't know, I never slept. I've never had bad feelings with neighbours. I've always minded my own business, and now I can't walk in the streets.

In District Six everyone would lend you things, do shopping for you, but in Mitchells Plain no one will lend you a match.

That morning Madam said: 'It is all the fault of forcing you people away from your real home.'

The next day Sarah went to the shop to buy food, then she started making supper for the twins. There was a knock at the door and this woman's son said: 'Why were you rude to my mother, why did you swear at her?'

'Don't talk rubbish,' Sarah said and tried to close the door.

His brothers arrived, charging into our house, breaking things, smashing our glass door, our furniture, throwing stones and bricks. I hid in an inside room, taking the little ones with me. Luke and Matthew came home and kicked one of the brothers to the ground, then they took stones and threw them at the other men.

They went home, then, but one man's shoe was in our lounge. Our house was a wreck. I was shaking so much I could not even make Sarah a cup of tea, she was just sobbing.

An hour later police arrived and they tell us to be at the police station at 4.30 am. Matthew and Luke have just gone to bed, and the police take them, dragging them in their pyjamas, throwing them into the police van like criminals, without a warrant of arrest, and put them in jail.

Sarah and I leave the house in the morning in pitch darkness, first taking the twins in that cold and dark to a relative. We had far to walk and carry those twins.

We all four were now out of work.

Sarah could not go to the clothing factory and was afraid they would sack her. Matthew missed going on the trawler and was out of work for three months because of this business.

We waited at the police station from 4.30 am. An hour later the policeman we were waiting for came.

At 8 am he told us we could go home but to return that evening. There was no one to leave the twins with, I had to get Sarah's husband to take them to his mother.

We walk all the way home. We have had nothing to eat or drink. I phone Madam, she is very upset.

At 7 pm that night we are back again at the police station and they put Sarah and me in jail. Poor Sarah was so nervous. As for me, I have never cried so much in my life, I have never done anything wrong, I have worked for over thirty years, I have never stolen, never owed money, never been drunk, and to see my daughter in the cell and us with a woman who stole a television set, another who killed her friend, another who stabbed her husband . . .

They gave us blankets, some brown bread and jam and black coffee. There was a toilet and a basin and no towel. We have no clothes because we never knew we would be kept.

The following day they allow me to phone Madam, she says she will phone an attorney. Next thing they told us we could go, but we must appear in court in the morning, so the next morning we're back again, all four of us, Sarah, Matthew, Luke and me. They give us R50 bail each.

Where could we get two hundred rands?

I phone Madam again. She said: 'Hettie I will get the money to you.'

'But it is 10.30 am and the money must be at the court by noon.'

'Be calm Hettie, I promise I will help you.'

But she, Madam, wasn't calm, I could hear that, and time was running out. I did not know if she would manage.

Sarah's husband didn't go to work either that morning. He was at court. Then he and my sons' friends all got together and went round to everyone they knew to collect for us. Luke's girlfriend's mother took out twenty cents from her purse – all she had.

Everyone chipped in. In two hours they managed to get the money. With all the ten cent pieces, twenty cent pieces, they got it. Luke's girlfriend got it all together and she comes and signs for us and we are out.

The case is remanded for a month. Meanwhile we see the lawyer twice, all four of us had to go to his office in town.

A month later we get to court, we sit and sit waiting for our case to come up. All of us were there, including the neighbours. Then all of a sudden they just said: 'The case is dropped.'

All that time and money wasted.

Outside the court the woman who started it all, she and her husband came up to us and said they dropped the case by themselves.

All the damage was on our property. We had to replace everything – even our beds were smashed up, but we got no compensation. Their house was untouched.

There is so much that is not right here in Mitchells Plain. The municipal workers are moving the ground and it's piled up in front of my house. I don't know when they will take it away and the wind blows and it brings all the sand into the house.

Those neighbours have no piles of sand in front of their house. I see them joke with the workers on the lorries, I see them have tea together. They have money . . . they get pensions . . .

It is hard here, certain people are pals, and if you are not one of them, you haven't got a chance.

I have nothing to do with my neighbours. In District Six people never fought with one another, no one ever went to jail because of a neighbour. Maybe there would be trouble from other parts, but not with us in District Six.

I don't look at my garden any more. Me, who loved flowers so much, it's all just sand again.

I who was the wildest in the family, so happy, so lively, skipping and jumping and laughing, am in low spirits all the time.

I don't want to think about the days when we all sat on our stoeps in District Six calling to each other, visiting, wishing each other on holidays, sharing meals, laughing and gossiping together.

Here you feel hate.

17 Hard times

I am stuck with a bill of R450 from the lawyer. I am glad we got out of that jail, but we all lost work and my nerves are so bad now.

After we got out, I didn't phone Madam. I just went to work at the usual time next morning. I couldn't look at her, my eyes were swollen, I was so humiliated.

She made coffee. I could hardly hold the cup. She makes me sit, and I tell her everything.

'It's not so bad for me to sit in jail, or Matthew and Luke – but Sarah . . . My poor Sarah . . .'

And my house broken, my garden trampled, the furniture wrecked. I have no insurance.

And all because we are not still in William Street. It seems it is always us coloureds who must carry the load.

Madam says: 'Hettie, I will recite a famous speech from The Merchant of Venice, it is Shylock's speech and it could be about South Africa.'

Afterwards I ask her to copy it out for me. It goes like this:

'I am a Jew! Hath not a Jew eyes? Hath not a Jew hands, organs, dimensions, senses, affections, passions? Fed with the same food, hurt with the same weapons, subject to the same diseases, healed by the same means, warmed and cooled by the same winter and summer as a Christian is? If you prick us, do we not bleed? If you tickle us, do we not laugh? If you poison us, do we not die? And if you wrong us, shall we not revenge? If we are like you in the rest, we will resemble you in that.'

Then Madam reads me other things about the Jews that could be about us in South Africa.

She says: 'Don't become bitter, Hettie – don't get warped.'

Like a record . . .

Suddenly I laugh. I say: 'Do you remember that old song, I'm gonna wash that man right out of my hair? Well, I'm going to wash those people right out of my mind. The government, too.'

There's a teacher Sarah knows, he's good with statistics and things

and he says that by the year 2000 there will be three times as many coloured people in the Western Cape as whites, so I think, Who will have the power then? Maybe one of my grandchildren will be a leader of the new province from Cape Point to the Little Karoo, and northwards to the Orange River. Maybe we'll go back to District Six? I tell Madam, and I laugh.

Much later that day Madam takes me to the station and I ask her to drive up to District Six. 'I just want to see the place, I have never been back.'

She sat in the car and pretended to read till I returned and said: 'Let's go to the station now.'

It's funny, apartheid is like a disease, it is like cancer, it comes slowly and people didn't take notice, and then suddenly it just hits you. Like when Ruby and Sammy were stopped by the police, we didn't realise how apartheid was starting then.

As we drove away I said: 'Did you see that couple who looked at me just now, as if to say, What are you doing here? I feel like saying to those Boere, I lived here once. But that type understands nothing, they don't even know to smile, they are not like the whites who used to live in District Six.'

My Dadda always walked straight, as if he's in a steel box. I don't know why I should think about him now, except if he was walking to pay for something he didn't do and he knew he was innocent, he'd walk proud.

So I walk proud and I'm going to the attorney's rooms and I'm at the desk ready to pay my tenth instalment. The secretary is writing out my receipt. I hear someone say:

'Hettie, maar kyk hoe smart is jy!'

I know that voice.

'Lizzie! What are you doing here?'

She is also paying off a case.

When we get outside we have a little chat. I could not believe that was Lizzie. She had turned out rotten, shop lifting.

'Hettie, I didn't want to leave William Street so I went and lived with the Africans on the corner, you remember at the bottom of the road, that building? Remember it was a whole mixed lot there, coloureds and Africans? But no one said those days, You are a kaffir, or this or that, we were all happy together in the street, all the same. Well, the Africans still had their rooms long after the coloureds left. Then I got pregnant, and now look at me.'

She had also sat in jail, Lizzie. She was broke, lonely, separated from those happy dronkies of William Street. 'I wonder Lizzie, where all those from your lane landed up?' I asked.

'My Ma went to Manenberg and I stayed on in Cannon Street till they threw us out. My Ma was so lonely; my Pa died, and she didn't last long after that. My sisters are charring. Hettie, do you remember our beautiful school? And the singing classes we all liked so much? And Hettie, do you remember when I got you lost?'

I am sure I will bump into Lizzie again – we both have to pay off for a long time.

Sometimes I go to church in Mitchell's Plain. The church is very small, and the altar's empty. There's a table and a tiny statue hanging over it, that's all.

In Districk Six we had a tall stone church, it was like a cathedral and there were lots of statues, beautiful ones. The choir sounded like angels in that church.

Here the choir can't even sing, they're so out of tune. It doesn't make you feel like you're in a church. In St Mark's it felt holy.

And here the people go just anyhow, in sloffies. They get dressed and go to church, there's nothing special in it, nothing at all.

18 Life goes on

All Friday I keep dropping things. Madam says: 'What is wrong with you Hettie?'

'I dreamed last night about a garden with a deep hole in it. What do you think it means?'

'I don't know Hettie, I'm not superstitious.'

'It is something bad.'

Saturday morning Ruby's daughter came to our house: 'Cilla is dead. She died at eight o'clock last night.'

I had not seen Cilla for years, but I knew that two of my brothers had gone to live with her. Kevin lives with her inbetween escorting cars to Durban.

Ruby's daughter told us the funeral would be on the Tuesday, meanwhile we all had to go to Cilla's house.

So Saturday afternoon I went to Cilla's house. It was the first time I had ever been there. It was in old Belhar. Her husband died six years ago, but her whole family was there, she had five children.

All of us were there, with our wives, husbands, children; and so many people from District Six too, those who got the message Cilla had died. I will never get used to the new names of our people. TV names, like Quinton, Meryl, Daryl. I still think of Rosies, Lizzies, Okkies, names like that. Cilla's children have all got smart names, and they are different. I don't know them. Even Rosie said she was a stranger there. In William Street I would have know them all, and they would have mixed with us and been friendly.

Tea came and there were cookies and cake for all the people. I didn't recognise my own family. Stan got cross with me because I said I saw him jolling in town, he said I was making trouble.

The day of the funeral everyone we knew who was still alive came from William Street. It is wonderful how they got the news and came.

Kevin told the driver of the hearse to wait in the street so they could carry the coffin from the house to the car. All my brothers carried the coffin, and one of Cilla's sons. Kevin didn't want to let go of the coffin.

After the funeral we all went to Cilla's house again. Noreen was

there, and it's funny, she told me she married and had only one daughter, and that daughter is twenty-two. I remembered our dreams and plans, the ones we made up as we lay under our green curtain. I never married but I have three children, so neither of us had our dreams come true.

'Haai, Hettie, did you hear old Amina married her priest?'

'You remember how we hated her in that street? She was like an exile.'

'And the other Cilla, she went to live in England. That Malay husband died and then after her son was hanged she married a proper whitey and left this country.'

I saw my brother Okkie at the funeral too. I hadn't seen him for years.

'Ken jy nie vir Okkie nie?' he asked me.

He looked bad, really bad – so thin and old. And he was only just older than me. He said his life was upside down, his wife lies in bed and never eats. People come and give her dops.

She used to be the cleanest girl I knew. I remember in District Six she pulled up her nose at others. Now she is one of those dirty ones, a dronkie.

Okkie came to live with me. He looks better already. I make him eat porridge and he is not drinking. I make him wash, and he sleeps well.

He loves TV. He sits in front of the TV till it ends, he doesn't move from there, so he won't go home.

When Luke comes home there's trouble. He wants that chair, so I must get another chair and shift them both so they can see the same. Then Okkie can be glued to the TV and Luke won't worry.

Sometimes Sarah also gets cross with Okkie when he doesn't look after her twins properly. He loses a slipper, burns out a kettle . . . and as soon as I get home he looks in my face and says: 'I'm off duty now.' Then I must see to the twins.

Even I get cross with Okkie. The other day I came home tired and that night I'm longing to get into bed and be warm, it was raining all day. And what did Okkie do? He decided to wash my blankets and they're still hanging outside in the rain.

It is five o'clock in the morning. I warm some water for the bucket so I can wash. I don't put electricity on, it costs too much for bath water.

I wash and I make sandwiches for Luke and porridge for him and the twins and Okkie. Matthew has gone off to sea.

Sarah must see to the twins before she goes to work, she has to tell Okkie what he must do for them during the day. She works a long day. I make coffee for her and take it to her bed.

Then I get myself ready. I put on my green skirt and blouse and yellow doek. I've got a long walk to the station.

I get myself all tensed up for the train, but the bus I like. I see people from District Six days and hear gossip. We have all changed so much from those days.

Sometimes on the bus whiteys sit there and I hear them say: 'We will have to learn to live with them.'

In District Six we didn't have to learn anything – we lived together and mixed happily together. Then I know that it's they who have a problem, not us.

I have a cup of tea when I get to work, then I go to the back toilet and have a cigarette. After that I change into my overall and start cleaning up. Later I have some breakfast, put on the radio, do the ironing. I read the newspapers and I don't understand what is going on in this country.

I can do nothing about it. Where can I go? Where can I take my children? Who will have us? What have we got?

The struggle of my life goes on and on, and I think: None of this would have happened if I still lived in William Street.

I don't know how to say it, but life is like a window, like there is glass in front of me, like those days when Okkie and me looked down through the glass roof into our diningroom.

Life is there, but something stops me.